Worshipping the Triune LORD

CARN BREA MEDIA

Worshipping the Triune LORD
ISBN 978-1-291-26831-7
© 2013 Stephen Dray & Gareth Leaney / Carn Brea Media
stephenpauldray@yahoo.co.uk

Worshipping the Triune God

Introduction

It is the incredible privilege of Christians to know and serve the God who has made himself known to human beings as Father, Son and Holy Spirit. The studies that follow are intended to help us know this God better and to learn to love and worship him. The studies have been prepared for those who attend Ferndale Baptist Church, Southend-on-Sea, but the authors hope that they will be of help to others as they seek to worship the true God.

Stephen Dray and Gareth Leaney, January 2013

1. We Believe God Can Be Known

While many deny the existence of God or that he can be known, the Christian believes that the LORD is God and has reveals himself in nature, the events of human history, in individual consciences and, above all, in the Bible.

Some people deny that God exists (These people are known as atheists). Others say that they believe God may exist but they do not think that he can be known or recognized (They are known as agnostics). But the Bible tells us that God can be and is known. The apostle Paul teaches this when he says "He has always given evidence of his existence" (Acts 14:17).

The LORD is known

1) **In the world that He has made**. In Romans 1:20 we read, "Ever since God created the world, his invisible qualities, both his eternal power and his divine nature, have been clearly seen..." As we reflect on the created world we should find evidence of God.

2) **In His ordering of the lives of humans and the activities of the nations**. We read, "From one man he made every nation of humans, that they should inhabit the whole earth; and he determined the times set for them and the exact places where they should live. God did this so that they would seek him and perhaps reach out for him and find him, though he is not far from each one of us." (Acts 17:26-7). When we consider own lives, we should detect evidence of his guidance.

3) **In the consciences of men and women**. In Romans 2:14-15 we read about people who do not know about God's written words but "do by nature the things required by the law (God's words)". This, we are told, shows, "That the requirements of the law (God's words) are written on their hearts, their consciences also bearing witness and their thoughts now accusing, now even defending them". Our consciences should teach us that God exists and is a good God who sets standards by which we should live.

Thus, God speaks in every aspect of our lives. Because this is true, this also explains why the Bible says, "The fool says in his heart, 'There is no God'" (Psalm 14:1 and 53:1). The word for 'fool' in these passages means someone who may be very clever but who has deliberately closed his or her mind to God and his teaching. Only the person who will not face the evidence can ever deny that God exists and can be known.

Listening to God

1) **The Bible teaches us that men and women customarily resist God's revelation**. This is clearly taught in Romans 1:21-28. Verse 21 emphasises this; "They know God, but they do not give him the honour that belongs to him, nor do they thank him (for making himself known). Instead, their thoughts have become complete nonsense, and their empty minds are filled with darkness". Human beings deliberately evade the truth and make fools of themselves by the arguments they use to deny it.

2) **We must be careful to listen for God's voice**. Otherwise, we are told, "Be careful, then, how you listen; because whoever has something will be given more, but whoever has nothing will have taken away from him even the little he

thinks he has"(Luke 8:18). If we listen, God will show us more of himself. If we won't listen he will take away that knowledge that we once had.

3) **So the Bible tells us that God speaks to us in every aspect of our lives**. However (as the statement above teaches), such knowledge is inadequate. Enough is revealed "so that men are without excuse" (Romans 1:20) when they reject such knowledge. But more is needed for us to come to know God personally.

4) **However, God has spoken clearly to us in the words of the Bible**. Jesus himself said of the Bible, "Your word is truth" (John 17:17). It is reliable and sufficient for all our needs.

5) **It is not enough, however, simply to read the Bible and to know everything that is in it**. We need God's Holy Spirit to show us the true significance and relevance of the words we read. Speaking of God's revelation, Paul said, 'we have received the Spirit who is from God, that we may understand what God has freely given us' (1 Corinthians 2:12).

Points to Ponder

- Since all this is true it is very important for us to give thought to God. He does exist and he can be known.
- We need to realise how important Bible Study and Bible teaching are.
- We need to pray that the Holy Spirit will teach us so that we can understand what we are reading.
- If we do this we will come to a fuller knowledge of God and, if we do not yet know him, will come to do so.

God speaks in the words of the Bible

As we read the words of the Bible we can be confident that all we read is God's truth because:

1) **It is inspired by him**. This is clearly taught in 2 Timothy 3:16 where we read, "All Scripture is God-breathed". Just as we use our breath to make speech-sounds so the Bible is God's speech: all of it.

2) **It is fully inspired**. This is also taught in 2 Timothy 3:16. Every part of the Bible is equally inspired. This does not mean that every part is equally important but it does mean that the whole of it is necessary to give us a full understanding of God and his message to us.

3) **It is verbally inspired**. This means that the individual words, though they are the words of the people who wrote the books are also God's words. In Amos 1:1 we are told that the book is "The words of Amos". In Hosea 1:1 "the word of the Lord was (spoken) to Hosea. Men's words are God's words. In Exodus 4:14-16 God says that Moses is to put words into the mouth of Aaron "as if you were God unto him".

4) **It is without error**. The Bible claims that God's words are authentic and true in all the claims they make. Jesus accepted everything as true (see Mark 10:16; Luke 11:51; Matthew 10:15; John 8:58; Luke 11:31,32; Matthew 22:43). This applied to history as well as other things and included those things that people deride or are most likely to , doubt! [This does not mean that we have answers to all the criticisms made of the Bible. It does, however, mean that in the vast majority of cases we can provide an answer to the charge that the Bible contains mistakes and on the basis of this we can be confident of the reliability of those passages for which we do

not yet have the answer.

5) **This inspiration applies only to the 39 Books of the Old Testament and the 27 Books of the New Testament.** Over the centuries Christians have received as God's words those Old Testament books that Jesus accepted and have recognised that the 27 books of the New Testament are so different from any other books that have ever been written that they have added them to the Old Testament to form the Bible. The New Testament writings themselves recognise that Paul's writings have the same authority as the Old Testament. We see this in 2 Peter 3:15-16 where Peter speaks of Paul's writings and "the other Scriptures".

6) **God has spoken to men.** We have an obligation to receive these words and obey them. We are to do the truth. John tells us this in John 3:21 and 1 John 1:6. We should be passionate to read God's word and to obey it. This is what we mean by the authority of the Bible......and we cannot be selective. All of God's words, whatever they tell us about, are to be obeyed. This is as true of our conduct and church life as it is of what it teaches about the way of salvation

Points to Ponder

- Is the whole of our life and thought under the authority of God's words?

2. We believe the LORD is God and the LORD is three

The God who has revealed himself, the LORD in the Bible, has shown us a lot about himself and that while there is only one true God, he comprises three distinct persons.

Some people believe that there are many gods (they are called polytheists). However, the Bible says: "The gods of all other nations are nothings" (Psalm 96:5) - useless and non-existent is implied. Others believe that there is one God, but little can be known about him (such people are known as deists). Thus, the Athenians had an altar to "an unknown God" (Acts 17:23). Speaking to the Samaritan woman Jesus said, "you do not really know whom you worship" (John 4:22). But….

God is known in the Bible

1) Jesus said of those who had the Scriptures, "we…know whom we worship" (John 4:22).

2) The Bible tells us there is only one true or genuine God, the LORD of the Bible. In 1 Kings 18:39 the people of Israel are forced to admit this truth when they say, "The LORD is God; the LORD alone is God".

The Bible tells us a great deal about the LORD

He is:

1) **Eternal**. Moses says, "from everlasting to everlasting to everlasting you are God" (Psalm 90:1). God did. not have a beginning and he will not have an end.

2) **Living**. He is not dead, he does not sleep. In Psalm 121:4 we read, "The protector... never dozes off or sleeps". He is awake and active.

3) **Holy**. This means that he is distinct from all creatures. He is completely pure and perfect. This is best expressed in Isaiah 6:3. "Holy, holy, holy! The LORD Almighty is holy!" (In the Bible, repeating the word 'holy' emphasises how truly holy God is).

4) **Good**. God is often so described, as in Psalm 34:8. This links God's holiness with his:

5) **Love**. The Bible tells us God is love (1 John 4:8). This is seen in:

6) **Mercy**. His heart is moved by the needy. "He has shown his kindness by giving you rain from heaven and crops in their seasons". (Acts 14:17).

7) **Longsuffering**. He doesn't get quickly provoked by others. He is "slow to get angry". But he is

8) **Angry about all sin**. Since he is holy and always consistent he must hate all sin and evil. In Romans 1:18 we read, "God's anger is revealed...against all sin."

9) **Righteous**. All he does is perfectly right. David tells us this in Psalm 145:17 when he says, "The LORD is righteous in all he does".

10) **Just**. This means much the same. He is fair in all his dealings. He is "just in all his ways" (Deuteronomy 32:4). However, above all, he shows:

11) **Gracious**. God's love is supremely seen in his provision of his Son as the one who bears the penalty for his holy wrath against sinners. John 3:16 says: "For God loved the world so very much, that he freely gave his only Son, that whoever believes in him may not perish (under his anger), but have eternal life." This also emphasises the costliness of God's love. In all this, he is

12) **All powerful** (or omnipotent). This is clearly seen when God asks Abraham, "Is anything too hard for the LORD?" (Genesis 17:1). This question expects the answer, "No". Thus in Luke 1:37 we are told, "… there is nothing that God cannot do". This is especially true of God being able to give sinful people new life. Jesus teaches this in Mark 10:27 where he says that man cannot save himself but "everything is possible for God".

13) **All present** (omnipresent). This is seen, especially, in Psalm 139:1-12. In verse 7 David asks, "Where can I flee from your presence?" and then answers, "Nowhere" in verses 8-12.

14) **All wise**. God not only knows everything BUT is perfectly sensible in the use to which he puts this knowledge. We read of this in Isaiah 40:13 where the question is asked, "Who needed to teach the LORD as his wise man?" Again the answer expected is, "No-one".

15) **All-knowing** (omniscient).In Psalm 139:3 David says, "You are familiar with all my ways", including thoughts and. actions (see verses 1-6).

16) **Without limitations**. His thoughts and ways are deeper than we can ever probe or fully understand. Paul says, "Who can explain his decisions? Who can understand his ways?" (Romans 9:33).

17) **Without need to rely on others**. In Genesis 1:1 we are told "In the beginning, God...." In Acts 17:25 Paul says, "Nor does he need anything we can supply by working for him, since it is he himself who gives life and breath and everything else to everyone".

18) **Always consistent** (immutable). He is dependable. Malachi says, "I the LORD do not change". James says that God "does not change like shifting shadows". (Malachi 3:6 & James 1:17).

Points to Ponder

- The LORD is surely worthy of our worship, thanksgiving, praise and delight.
- The proper response to such a God must be to serve him in every area of our lives.
- Such a God ought to be shared with others who do not yet love him.

The Bible reveals that the one God is three persons: Father, Son and Holy Spirit

This may be difficult to understand but is taught clearly in the Bible and is very important to our understanding of the LORD and his relationship with us and our worship of him.

Thus, the Bible teaches that:

1) **The Father is God**. Paul speaks of "God the Father" in Galatians 1:1.

2) **The Son is God**. Paul speaks of "our great God and Saviour, Jesus Christ" in Titus 2:13. John 1:1 tells us that the Word (the Son) was God. These, and many other passages teach us that the Son is God. Those who deny this have to explain away the plain teaching of the Bible. We should also note that the Son is eternally God. Before anything was created He was already God (John 1:1). Just as God is eternal so is the Son.

3) **The Holy Spirit is God**. In 2 Corinthians 3:17-18 we read of "the Lord, who is the Spirit."

The Bible also teaches that:

1) **The Father is a person**. The language of the Bible regularly speaks of the Father in words that can only be true of persons not things. This is especially true when we are told of the Father's love for the world (in John 3:16) and for Jesus (in John 17:23). Things can't love, people can.

2) **The Son is a person**. In John 17 Jesus shows that he enjoyed a personal relationship with the Father from eternity.

3) **The Holy Spirit is a person.** The Holy Spirit is frequently spoken of as having personal characteristics. He can teach (John 14:26), be made sad (Ephesians 4:29). He can bear witness (John 15:26) etc. All these things can only be done by a person. The Holy Spirit is not just an influence.

Sometimes people try to confuse true Christians by denying that Jesus is God. They do this by

- Saying that since a son is born after a father, so the Son must have been created by the Father and therefore cannot be God. This is a clever argument but it refuses to take seriously what the Bible really says. When the Bible says that the second person of the Trinity is the 'Son', it means that he shares the same (divine) nature – just as a human father shares exactly the same human nature as his son. Thus to speak of the 'Son' does not deny that Jesus is God, rather it affirms it!

- Referring to those passages which speak of Jesus as 'junior' to the Father. But they confuse two things. Just as a father may be senior to his son and yet share the same nature, so Jesus shares the same nature as his Father although the Father is 'senior'.

3. We Believe in Creation

The one God, the LORD, Father, Son and Holy Spirit, is eternal: having no beginning or end and created and keeps everything.

All other things were made by him

1) **The Bible teaches that this was something done by both the Father and the Son:** "All things were made by God through the Son, and apart from him nothing was made that exists" (John 1:3).

2) **The Holy Spirit was also at work in God's work of creation:** "And the Spirit of God was moving (at work) over the waters" (Genesis 1:2).

He made everything without having anything from which to make it

1) In Hebrews 11:3 we read, "The universe was made at God's command, so that what is seen was made out of what was not visible", that is, from nothing.

2) God even created the world of spirits. So, in Psalm 148, we read, "Praise him, all His angels, all his heavenly armies. He commanded, and they were created' (verses 2, 5).

3) God made all things perfect. We are told, "God saw everything He had made, and it was perfect" (Genesis 1:31).

4) Men and women were part of this perfection. See, especially, Genesis 1:26-27. They were created able not to sin and free from death. Paul teaches this when he says, "sin entered the world through one man, and death through sin" (Romans 5:12).

God did not create everything and then leave it alone to run by itself

1) The Bible teaches that, **moment by moment, God creates new things, controls and supervises everything that He makes, and, that if He did not do so everything would go to pieces**.

   Referring especially to the Son we are taught in Hebrews 1:3: "He sustains all things by his powerful word' (that is, he keeps everything together). Then, in Colossians 1:17, we are taught the same thing, "in him all things hold together".

2) **So God makes new things.**

   He gives agricultural, technological and even military skills. Referring to the farmer, Isaiah says, "God instructs him" (28:26). Of the blacksmith God says, "it is I who created the blacksmith" (Isaiah 54:16). Speaking of warfare David said, "He trains my hand" (Psalm 144:1).

3) **God does things again and again**

   Day by day, "he brings out all the stars one by one" (Isaiah 40:26), season by season, he gives crops' (Acts 14:17), moment by moment "God clothes the grass" (Matthew 6:30). Thus the most insignificant as well as the greatest things are controlled by him, even the weather: "He sends rain..." (Matthew 5:45).

4) **He is in control of everything all the time.**

The Psalmist says, "Our God...does whatever he wishes" (115:3). This applies even to the smallest things, "even the hairs of your head have all been counted" (Matthew 10:30).The salvation of human beings is under God's full control. In Ephesians 1:11 we read, "All things are done according to God's plan and decision; and God chose us to be his people in union with Christ because of his own purpose, based on what he had decided from the very beginning". Even disasters are under God's control. Amos says, "When disaster comes to a city, has not the LORD caused it." (Amos 3:6). Evil may be used of God for his own ends. So in Acts 2:23 we read, "In accordance with his own will God had already decided that Jesus would be handed over to you".

The 'problem' of evil

The Bible recognises the problem of evil but it makes no attempt to give a full answer to the problem (if such were possible). Typically of the Scriptures it is more concerned to teach only what is necessary to guide the believer through his or her life of faith.

1) **It reminds us that evil is the result of humankind's sin and not part of God's original purpose.** See Romans 5:12.

2) **It emphasises that evil and suffering will not finally frustrate God's purpose.** In Revelation 21:4 we read, "He will wipe away all tears from their eyes. There will be no more death, no more grief or crying or pain. The old things have disappeared".

3) **It stresses that God uses evil and suffering to his glory.**

So Acts 2:23 noted above.

4) **It reminds us that God, in the person of his Son, was willing to enter himself into the full experience of sin and death.** He suffered unjustly and paid the ultimate penalty of injustice. Thus he can enter into our sufferings with great sympathy since the experiences of a human heart have now been taken up into God.

Points to Ponder

- 'The earth is the LORD's, and all that is in it' (Psalm 24:1). We should enjoy all of God's creation to the glory of God.
- We should humbly recognise our utter dependence on God.
- We should learn to be thankful for all His goodness to us.
- When we suffer for no fault of our own, we may be comforted that all our affairs are in the hand of a sovereign God of love.
- We can have great security in the midst of an insecure world.

4. We Believe in the Fall

God created all things perfect, but we live in a world that is far from perfect: a world full of wickedness, sorrow, disaster and death. How did this great change come about?

Man rejected God

In Genesis 3:1-6 we read of the sin of Adam and Eve in the Garden of Eden. We must be very clear that their sin did not lie so much in eating the forbidden fruit as in rebelling against and rejecting God. By eating, Adam and. Eve tried to snatch equality with God (verse 5) and to assert their independence of God. Moreover, they questioned God's loving provision for them and were ready to listen and follow the enemy of God, despite all that he had provided for them.

We need to learn this lesson. When we sin, the 'act' may seem small and insignificant to us: but behind such acts lies high treason in the heart against the sovereign LORD.

Sin has extended to all humankind

The Bible teaches that, "sin entered the world through one man ....and in this way death (which is the result of sin) came to all" (Romans 5:12). This is described in the Bible as the 'Fall' of humanity. The explanation of this is not easy but, what we can say is, it does explain the world as we now see and experience it.

Sin has affected every part of humankind

1) **Our actions are affected**. In Galatians 5:19-21 we read of, "Immorality, impurity, debauchery, idolatry, witchcraft, hatred, jealousy, fits of rage, selfishness."

2) **Our minds and understandings are affected**. So in Genesis 6:5 we learn, "The LORD saw ...man's wickedness that every inclination of the thoughts of his heart was only evil all the time".

3) **Our affections and emotions are damaged**. We learn about this in Romans 1:24 where we learn that because of sin, "God gave people over desires of their hearts".

4) **Our wills are affected**. Jesus said, "everyone who sins is a slave to sin" (John 8:54). Paul said, "all have sinned" (Romans 3:23).

5) **Our hearts are affected**. In the Bible the 'heart' is the 'core' of a person. Genesis 6:5 says, "the thoughts of everyone's heart was evil all the time".

6) **Sin has affected the whole of the created order**. God told Adam, "The ground is cursed because of you" (Genesis 3:17). Paul says, "The creation was made subject to frustration" (Romans 8:20).

The Consequences of the Fall

1) While we can and do accomplish 'good' things, yet **we can never achieve the lifelong perfection of our inner thoughts and our outward actions**. But this is what is necessary if we are ever to stand before God and not be condemned.

2) **We are unable to save ourselves**. Rotten at the core we have neither the will nor the strength to save ourselves.

3) Being unable to do God's will and incapable of hearing God's voice clearly **we are under His condemnation**. Paul said, "The judgment followed one sin and brought condemnation" (Romans 5:16).

4) **In ignorant fear of God, we try to make ourselves our own master**. Paul says, "He opposes and exalts himself over everything that is called God" (2 Thessalonians 2:4). We set our own standards and then claim God ought to accept us, excusing our own sinful ways.

5) **We are now turned against our fellow human**. Conflict, exploitation and misunderstanding sour even the best relationships. Adam turned against Eve, Cain against Abel (Genesis 3:12: 4:8).

6) **We are now incapable of judging ourselves properly**. Inner conflict, division and restlessness are the result. Says Isaiah, "the wicked are like the tossing sea which cannot rest ...There is no peace...for the wicked". (57:20) Self-love and self-rejection are two of the results.

7) **We cannot exercise authority over the creation properly**. Selfishness and ambition lead to exploitation and pollution.

8) **Subject to death we try to cling to passing pleasures.**

Points to Ponder

- The Bible is robust in its analysis of the world and its inhabitants! At the same time, it offers an explanation that faces us with an explanation of the world as we find it (not least the world of our hearts).

- Being honest, we should recognise ourselves described here. This prepares us for the next section.

5. We Believe in the LORD's Rescue Plan

Sinful human beings are unable to effect their own salvation since they are helpless arid incapable of either choosing or acting in a way which pleases God. Is our condition helpless? The Bible answers with a resounding 'No'.

In our helplessness God determined to act

1) Paul tells us, "When we were dead in trespasses and sins, God..." (Ephesians 2:4).

2) He did this without giving consideration to the quality of life or the sort of people for whom he would act. Paul also says, "It is by grace" (Ephesians 2:5, 8). Grace is unmerited. God determined to act not because of those he was acting for but despite them!

3) God planned to save specific individuals. Thus, He planned to do all that was necessary to effect the salvation of these helpless individuals. This is seen in Romans 8:29-30 where Paul tells us that those people God "foreknew" he, then, "destined in advance to be conformed to the image of His Son [and] those He called... justified ....and glorified".

4) Alongside such teaching the Bible tells us that all of us are held responsible for their sin and rejection of God. We read, "see to it that you do not refuse him who speaks. If they did not escape when they refused him who warned them on earth, how much less will we, if we turn away from him who warns us from heaven" (Hebrews 12:25).

5) All are commanded to freely receive God's salvation. Paul tells us, "God commands all people everywhere to repent" (Acts 17:30) and Peter adds, "God does not want anyone to perish, but everyone to come to repentance" (1 Peter 3:9).

Thinking about God's choice

It is not easy to understand how all these things can be true at the same time. However, the important thing is that these teachings help us make sense of our own experience. When the Gospel message was told us we were conscious of its demands upon us and we acted on the basis of what we heard (if we are believers). Thus, at Pentecost, Peter's hearers said "What shall we do." He told them, "Repent" and there were those who accepted his message and. did so (Acts 2:57-41).

And yet we need to ask ourselves the question, 'Why did. I believe, and not others?' Some who have heard the Christian message are nicer people with a better understanding of its teachings than we are or were but are still not believers. Why not? Why did we turn to seek God and not them? The only answer can be…God did it!

Points to Ponder

- These truths remind us of the glorious sovereignty of God over all things.
- They emphasise the greatness of His love toward us.
- They provoke true humility in the believer.
- They insist on our own responsibility for all we are or do.
- They remind us that we can trust Him when we feel helpless.

6. We Believe in God, the Son

The Son of God was LORD from all eternity. However, he became a human being in the person of Jesus Christ.

The Son of God became a Man

1) He had a body exactly like ours:

- After His remarkable conception (we explore this below) he developed in the womb like any other child. He was "made of a woman" (Galatians 4:4) and was born, as all are, "when the time came for the baby to be born" (Luke 2:6). He grew up just like any other child. Says Luke, "the child grew and became strong" (Luke 2:40).

- His body had the same limitations as ours. He became tired (John 4:6), "he was hungry" (Matthew 21:18), He experienced pain of mind, "sorrow to the point of death" (Matthew 14:34)] and body. So John says, "he became flesh" (John 1:14).

- He had a personality identical to ours. Thus, he experienced emotions like ours: He could be "full of joy" (Luke 10:21), "sorrowful and troubled" (Matthew 26:37) and "full of pity" (Matthew 9:36). He loved (John 11:5), was "amazed" (Luke 7:9) and knew anger (Mark 3:5). All these human experiences, He experienced.

2) Yet He remained fully God:

- He claimed to be the "I AM", the special name of God, the LORD (Exodus 3:14). He said, "I AM the bread of life" (John 6:35. see also John 8:12,24,58;11:25; 14:16;18:5 and Mark 14:62).

- Four of the apostles make the same claim. Thomas said, "My Lord and my God" (John 20:28). John speaks of him as "God the only Son" (John 1:18). Paul remarks that "Christ… is God over all" (Romans 9:5).Peter refers to "our God and Saviour Jesus Christ"(2 Peter 1:1).

3) All this evidence led the Christian Church to speak of the Lord Jesus as being 'one person with two natures': fully God and perfect man. They have thus denied that:

- Jesus was a mixture of the divine and human. Such a mixture would be neither God nor man but some sort of 'Superman'.
- Jesus was made up of bits and pieces of deity and humanity which were fused together. Such a Jesus would not be fully God nor perfect man.
- Jesus was not two persons loosely united but separable into two different persons- a sort of schizophrenic.
- Jesus was not a man absorbed into God so that he ceased to be fully man. This would deny his perfect humanity.
- The Church has thus confessed a mystery: His fully divine nature was united to a fully human one in a unity which cannot be broken - and yet He remains one person!

4) God became man through the virgin birth The Bible teaches clearly that Jesus was conceived in the womb of Mary, his mother, when she was still a virgin. His conception was effected by the Holy Spirit. So Matthew tells us, "Jesus' birth occurred in this way: when His mother Mary was engaged to Joseph, before they were married or had slept together, she was found to be pregnant of the Holy Spirit". (1:18) Luke tells us that she was a virgin (1:27) and quotes her words when she was told that she would be the mother of Jesus,

"How can this happen, because I have never slept with a man". (1:34). This is difficult to understand, but is clearly taught. Its significance is explained for us by Matthew. This means, he says, that "God is with us". (1:23).

Sometimes people who claim to follow the teaching of the Bible deny: 1) that the 'Son' was eternally God and, 2) that Jesus was fully God.

Such persons usually begin their arguments by claiming that to believe in a God who is one and yet three is illogical and this is not what the Bible teaches. For something to be illogical is different from saying that something is beyond the ability of the human mind to be grasped. The Christian claims the second.

However, three arguments are usually used to deny the Bible teaches that Jesus is the Son of God. It is said:

- Jesus speaks of Himself as inferior to the Father so he cannot be fully God. So in John 14:28 Jesus says, "My Father is greater than I". However, just as a human son can be 'less than' his father in dignity and yet fully share the same human nature so the same is true of Jesus and the Father. John 14:28 need not say more than this and, in the light of the rest of Scripture, must have such an explanation if the Scriptures are not to contradict themselves.

- Jesus is described in the Bible as "only begotten" (John 3:16), therefore, He must have come into existence after the Father existed and, therefore, is not eternally the Son. This argument sounds very plausible. However, the word translated 'only begotten' in our Bibles emphasises uniqueness rather than that something comes into being after something or someone else. And Jesus is unique.

- Jesus is described as "the firstborn of creation" (Colossians 1:15), therefore He must be one of God's creations. Again, the argument is plausible but does not ask the question, 'What did the word 'firstborn' mean in the language of the New Testament writers?' Since the answer to that question is, 'It meant 'head', the most likely meaning of such passages is that Jesus is head of Creation as its author.

7. We Believe in Jesus' Death and Resurrection for Us

The Bible teaches that the Son of God became a human being to die and rise again for us.

Why did God the Son become a human being like us?

To understand the Bible's answer it is helpful to know something about the Old Testament system of sacrifices. Especially in the Book of Leviticus, we read that God told Moses to institute the sacrifices; the most important of which took place on the Day of Atonement (Leviticus 16). These sacrifices were intended to teach that:

1) Acting contrary to God's revealed will for mankind places the individual under the holy anger of God and subject to death. Thus Paul says, "God's anger is revealed from heaven against all sin (so) sin pays its wage – death" (Romans 1:18; 6:23).

2) The absolute necessity of a perfect substitute to secure the favour and reconciliation of God.

- The idea of substitution is clearly stated in Leviticus 16:21 where we are told, "the sins and rebellions of the people... (were) transferred to the goat's head".
- The necessity of a perfect offering is seen in Leviticus 1:2,3 when God tells Moses, "anyone who offers an animal sacrifice... must bring (an animal) without any defects".

- That "sins are forgiven only if blood is poured out" (Hebrews 9:22).
- That such sacrifices were only effective when accompanied by a repentant heart. David recognised this when he said, 'you will not reject a humble and repentant heart' (Psalm 51:17).

3) Another important feature of the Day of Atonement was that the sacrifice was offered by the High Priest. As a mediator, he represented God's people before him and yet was, himself, a man like those for whom he sacrificed. This is expressed in Hebrews 5:1 where we are told, 'the high priest is selected from among men to represent them'.

4) This same idea of a close kinsman delivering someone in particular distress is found in the 'kinsman-redeemer' who is mentioned in Leviticus 25:48-49 and Ruth 4:1-15.

The New Testament teaches that:

1) "The blood of bulls and goats can never really take away our sins" (Hebrews 10:4). Rather,

2) The sacrificial system only applied "until the time God established the new order" (Hebrews 9:10).

3) The reason for this is that they all looked forward to the time when "Christ was offered in sacrifice once and for all time to take away the sins of many" (Hebrews 9:28).

4) Thus, Jesus, who was a true man was able to act as a High Priest and Kinsman-Redeemer:

- He was without sin. When He asked, "Which one of you can prove that I am guilty of sin?" (John 8:46) no-one could charge him.
- Thus he was able to, "offer one sacrifice for sins, an offering

that is effective for ever" (Hebrews 10:12).

- This he did for his own people. He said, "I know my sheep..... and I am willing to die for them" (John 10:15).
- His death achieves forgiveness and reconciliation. Paul says Jesus' death is "the means whereby... sins are forgiven" (Romans 3:25) and that 'God made us his friends through the death of his Son' (Romans 5:10).
- Jesus did this by his righteousness being reckoned to his people and their guilt being reckoned to Him.

5) The benefits of Jesus' death are personally appropriated by repentance and faith. Peter told the crowd of Jerusalem "Repent" (Acts 2:38) and. Paul at Philippi said, "Believe in the Lord Jesus, and you will be saved" (Acts 16:31).

This same Jesus rose from the dead, bodily, and ascended into heaven

The Bible insists that Jesus was raised bodily from the tomb. This fact is emphasized by:

1) **The empty tomb.** We read, "They found the stone rolled away from the entrance to the tomb, they went in; but they did not find the body of Jesus" (Luke 24:2, 3).

2) **His having a body** which had flesh and bones (Luke 24:39); which could be touched (John 20:27), and eat (Luke 24:43).

The Bible also insists that Jesus' body had new properties. Above all, it was no longer subject to death and the effects of mortality. This truth is spelt out in 1 Corinthians 15 where the final condition of believers is grounded in the resurrection of Jesus: they will be free from corruption and death because he is.

A number of practical lessons for the believer are rooted in the teaching of the resurrection of Jesus:

1) **Jesus' bodily resurrection proves that he is God**. God alone gives life for it was he who 'breathed life-giving breath into....man (Genesis 2:7). Jesus claimed equality with God. When he said, ' I am the resurrection and the life' (John 11:25) and argued, 'Just as the Father raises the dead and gives them life, in the same way the Son gives life to those he wants to' (John 5:21). This claim he proved true by rising from the dead, 'a life-giving Spirit' (1 Corinthians 15:45).

2) **Jesus' resurrection tells us that the Father has accepted his offering for sin**. Paul says, "He was raised to life for (to prove) our having been put right with God" (Romans 4:25). Thus, he also says, "Who can condemn us? Not Christ Jesus, for he was raised to life" (Romans 8:34).

3) **Jesus' resurrection proves that He has conquered sin, death and the demonic world**. Thus:

- "He was offered in sacrifice once (since he was resurrected and is now ascended) to take away the sins of many" (Hebrews 9:28).
- "He has ended the power of death and through the gospel has revealed immortal life" (2 Timothy 1:10).
- "(God) raised Christ from death and seated him at his right side in the heavenly world. Christ rules there above all heavenly rulers, authorities, powers, and lords; he has a title superior to all titles of authority in this world and the next" (Ephesians 1:20, 21).

4) **Jesus' resurrection guarantees the resurrection of believers into the final reign of Christ**. So Paul says, "Christ has been raised from death, as the guarantee that those who sleep in death will also be raised" (1 Corinthians

5:20). Thus, "we wait for what God has promised: new heavens and a new earth, where righteousness will be at home" (2 Peter 3:13).

The Bible also teaches that Jesus ascended into heaven, bodily. Luke tells us, "He was taken up to heaven, as His disciples watched Him, and a cloud hid him from their sight" (Acts 1:9).

There are a large number of practical lessons that we can draw from the ascension of Jesus:

1) **Jesus' ascension confirms his divine nature.** In both the Old Testament (Exodus 40:34) and the New Testament (Luke 9:34-35) the cloud is a symbol of God's glory and presence. So when Jesus was received into the cloud his divine nature is confirmed.

2) **Jesus' ascension declares that he is now Lord and King over all.** This is since, "God has raised him to the highest place" (Philippians 2:9), that is, "at God's right hand - with angels, authorities and powers in submission to Him" (1 Peter 3:22).There, he is "crowned with glory and honour" (Hebrews 2:9).

3) **Jesus' ascension guarantees that we work for a victorious Lord.** This should give us great confidence and assurance in our work for the Lord.

4) **Jesus' ascension guarantees or future glory.** Jesus reigns, "until he has put all his enemies under his feet" (1 Corinthians 15:25). Thus, we labour on with our eyes fixed upon our future and great reward.

5) **Jesus' ascension gives us great security in an insecure world**, since, "All authority is given to me" (Matthew 2:18).

6) **Jesus' ascension is a ground for great comfort.**

7) **Jesus' ascension guarantees the resources for all our Christian living and service.** "The promised Holy Spirit he has poured out" (Acts 2:33) as a result of his ascension. Ascended, he has poured out gifts upon his church (see Ephesians 4:8-12) and has put at the church's disposal nothing less than the power which resurrected Jesus from the dead and then put him at God's right hand. We read about this in Ephesians 1:19, 20.

Points to Ponder

- Go back over the last section and note how much that is said applies directly to you!
- As you reflect upon each point, consider how believing these things should shape and change your life.

8. We Believe in the Holy Spirit

How can sinful men and women who are incapable of any spiritual good benefit from the work that Jesus did for them? The answer that the Bible gives is that the Holy Spirit is our helper, doing what we cannot do.

The Holy Spirit brings us to Jesus

The Holy Spirit:

1) **Calls**. The Bible does speak of a call which God makes to all who hear the Gospel message. Jesus tells us that, "many are called, but few are chosen" (Matthew 9:13). But the Bible also talks about a 'call' which is always effective. This is especially clear in Romans 8:29 and 30. Paul says, "Those God foreknew, he called... justified... glorified". When the Gospel is preached some respond... because of the Spirit's call.

2) **Regenerates**. Men and women are spiritually dead. Just as a dead person cannot do anything so a spiritually dead person cannot do anything spiritual. So he cannot either repent or believe the Gospel. But the Holy Spirit is able to give spiritual life: when this happens a person is described as being "born of the Spirit" (John 3:5).

When a child is born it automatically does certain things: it breathes, cries, feeds without ever being taught. The same is true of spiritual birth. In particular, two things follow:

- Repentance in which a person turns from sin to Christ. So Jesus told his hearers, "Turn away from your sins and believe the Gospel" (Mark 1:15). John tells us that repentance is absolutely necessary to true belief when he says, "Whoever is a child of God does not continue to sin" (1 John 3:9).
- Faith. Faith is not mere belief in the truth of the Gospel message. Devils believe (James 2:19) but they do not have faith:

  - o Faith is personal commitment to the Gospel of Jesus.
  - o Faith is trust in the truth of that Gospel.
  - o Faith, then, is personal trust in the Gospel and the one revealed in the Gospel. It is essential for, "without faith it is impossible to please God" (Hebrews 11:6). It is the result of God's grace (see Ephesians 2:8) and the work of his Spirit.

3) **Unites us to Christ**. Faith and repentance bring all the blessings of salvation purchased by Jesus for his people.

In particular we are now reckoned as.

1) **Justified**. We are reckoned as free from the debt we owe to God as a result of our sin. Paul says that "Being justified by faith, we have peace with God through our Lord Jesus Christ" (Romans 5:1).

2) **Adopted children of God**, installed within the intimacy of the family circle of our Heavenly Father. This means:

  - We now know the creator God as 'our own dear Father'. Paul tells us, "by the Spirit's power we cry out to God, 'Father, my Father'" (Romans 8:15). This is a great comfort in prayer.

- We are now part of the family of God, the Church.
- Jesus is now our 'older brother': He is "the first among many brothers" (Romans 8:29). This is marvellous! We are given the same status with God as that of the Lord Jesus!
- We are now sure that, 'God will give (us) all that He has for His sons' (Galatians 4:6).

The continuing work of the Holy Spirit

Every part of this work of 'conversion' is undertaken by the Holy Spirit. But that does not end his work in and for the believer. Rather, he continues his work in every believer:

1) **He gives us assurance that we are truly God's children**. This He does in three ways:

- Since faith is His work alone, faith itself is a ground for assurance.
- He produces that spiritual life which alone can be accomplished by those in whom He is at work.
- He "bears witness to our spirits that we are the children of God" (Romans 8:16) giving us an inward assurance that Christ is ours.

We should never depend on the last alone for without the second we have no certainty that we are not deluding ourselves with a false faith and a secure 'feeling'. Sometimes the witness disappears. This can be because of our sins and we should search ourselves in such circumstances. On other occasions it mysteriously disappears for no apparent reason. When this happens we should look to the first two for our comfort.

2) **He makes us holy**. The Holy Spirit produces a moral transformation in all God's people: this is to be expected since he is God's Holy Spirit. Thus:

- He produces the 'fruit of the Spirit' in us: "love, joy, peace, patience, kindness, goodness, faithfulness, humility and self-control" (Galatians 5:22, 23).
- He gives gifts to every member of his children so that they may strengthen one another. Paul says, "When he went up to heaven....... he gave gifts .... in order to build up the body of Christ" and, he adds, "Each one of us has received a special gift" (Ephesians 4:8,12 and 7).

3) **He keeps us**. This he does by:

- Giving us the wisdom we need to live to God's glory day by day. We are told, "If any of you lacks wisdom, he should pray to God, who will give it to him" (James 1:5).
- Meeting God's people again and again as they have need (see especially Acts 4:23-31, especially 31).
- Ensuring our safe passage to glory. He is described as: the first-fruits (Romans 8:23). or, the 'taster' of our eternal life; the down-payment, or, guarantee (Ephesians 1:14). Thus he is the first instalment of God's promise.

All this he accomplishes through the Bible. The Bible was written by, "Men...under the control of the Holy Spirit" (2 Peter 1:21). So, when we quote the Bible we can say, "the Holy Spirit says" (Hebrews 3:7). It is the Holy Spirit who helps us to understand the Bible. John says, "You have had the Holy Spirit poured out on you by Christ, and. so all of you understand the truth" (1 John 2:20). And that Word is able to guide, inspire, make holy and build up God's people (see 2 Timothy 3:16).

Point to Ponder

- Without the personal ministry of the Holy Spirit, we could never have come to faith or sustained our Christian life and growth. Wow!

9. We Believe in Jesus' Return

Salvation from sin was planned by the Father, accomplished by Jesus, the Son and is applied to us by the Holy Spirit. However, the results of the Fall are still with us. How can this be? The answer given by the Bible is that the full display of God's salvation still lies in the future.

Understanding our Future Hope

To understand what the Bible says about the future it is first necessary to find out what the Bible means when it talks about the 'Kingdom of God' or the 'Kingdom of Heaven'.

1) **The words, 'the Kingdom of God' were often on the lips of Jesus**. We see this in Matthew 12:28; Mark 1:14; 9:1; Luke 13:18-20 and John 3:3. When we speak about a kingdom we usually refer to a geographical place. This is not true of the Bible. There 'kingdom' means rule that is seen in action. This is very clear in Psalm 145:13. The first half of the verse speaks about God and says: "Your rule is eternal and you are king I or ever". The second half of the verse explains what this means: "The LORD is faithful to His promises and everything he does is good".

   This shows that God's kingship is seen in the things he does. He is active and always at work. With this in mind it is helpful to turn to the Old. Testament.

2) **In the Old Testament God was seen as king over everything**. So we read:

"The LORD is king...
The earth is set in place so firmly
That it cannot be moved
Your throne, O LORD, has been firm from the beginning
and you existed before time began...
For the LORD is a mighty God
a mighty king over all the gods" (Psalms 93:1,2; 95:3).

3) **However, because of sin, God is resisted and opposed by the Devil.** The result of this is that the Old Testament people of God, both as individuals and together, discovered a great, almost unbearable, tension in their experience.

- They lived in a world in which hostility existed between humans and the rest of Creation. They knew that "while the sweat is still pouring off your forehead you will have to eat" (Genesis 3:19).
- They also knew the reason for such hard work: "(the earth) will produce thorns and thistles" (Genesis 3:18) In other words, they found the Creation constantly frustrating them. So much so that one of them repeatedly said:

  > "It is pointless, pointless.....
  > Life is pointless" (Ecclesiastes 1:1, etc.).
  > The reason for this was: "You spend your life working, labouring, and. what do you have to show for it" (Ecclesiastes 1:2).

- The Old Testament believers also recognised a hostility which existed between human beings. They knew that it was not only Cain who felt like saying: "Am I my brother's keeper" (Genesis 4:9).
- The Old Testament saints also knew of inner disquiet: "Why are you downcast? Why so disturbed within me?" (Psalm 42:5).

Thus in every area of life there was a contradiction between their experience and the kingship of God.

4) **Into this experience and, situation the prophets spoke.** They said that one day, called "The Day of the Lord" (Amos 5:18 etc.), God would show that he really was the king of everything. He would put everything right. They expected God to do this through his Messiah: a great ruler who would sort out the whole sorry mess by conquering once and for all the Devil. We see this hope expressed in Isaiah 9:6, 7. Genesis 3:15 was also seen as referring to the conquest of the 'Prince' of Evil. When all this happened 'Paradise' would be restored. We see this vividly described in Amos 9:13-15.

5) **When we turn to the New Testament we learn that Jesus taught two things about the 'Day of the Lord' or 'the Kingdom of God':**

- He taught that he had brought the Kingdom into being. So in Mark 1:15 he said, "the Kingdom of God has arrived". God's reign had begun, he said, as men and women understood the significance of his words and ministry. As by faith they received Him they would enter into the experience of 'eternal life' or 'the Kingdom of God'. So they would experience something of "the age to come" (Hebrews 6:5). They would know victory over sin (1 John 3:9): "No- one who is born of God will habitually sin".

  They would also experience the power of Christ, especially in fellowship: "(he) is able to do immeasurably more than all we ask or think, according to his power at work in us" (Ephesians 3:20). This would be seen, especially in spiritual growth and grace (the context of Ephesians).

- He also taught that the Kingdom had not yet fully arrived. So the New Testament writers teach that creation still remains hostile to mankind. Paul in Romans 8:18-27 expresses this. The curse on Creation still remains. Hostility still, exists between men: especially between the children of the Kingdom and others. Luke 21:12 makes this especially clear. Inner turmoil still exists. Says Paul: "For what I do is not the good I want to do; no, the evil I do not want to do - this I keep on doing" (Romans 7:19).

Bruce Milne puts it like this:

> "(Thus) the tension between these two dimensions is in the context of the Christian life. On the one hand, the Christian is a new person, united with Christ in his death, resurrection and reign, and sharing the powers of the new age of the kingdom in the Holy Spirit; on the other hand, the old nature is still a painful and persistent reality, dragging Christians below the moral attainments to which their new life directs them.

> "Thus we rejoice in the coming of the kingdom, in the fact of eternal salvation, in the blessings of the new age in our union with Christ; and. yet we long for our deliverance, the final coming of the kingdom, the completion of our salvation and the full emergence of the new man in Christ."

The Return of Jesus

In the Bible the final coming of the Kingdom is identified with the return of the Lord Jesus Christ.

At Jesus' return:

1) **The dead will be raised to life**. In answer to the question, 'What is humanity?' the Bible says that humans are, first of all, material bodies. So Genesis 2:7 tells us that "God formed man from the dust of the ground" - that is, from the same chemical elements that make up our material world.

The Bible also teaches that we are only truly human when our bodies are filled with God-given life. This is why we are told, "God breathed into man's nostrils the breath of life and man became a living being" (Genesis 2:7).

However, sin has affected humanity and death now intervenes. Thus God said, "Dust you are and to dust you will return" (Genesis 3:19). This is a fact that we are all frequently confronted with.

The Bible tells us that this does not mean the end for humans. The God-given life principle does continue without the body. It is known as the 'soul' or 'spirit' of man. This is why John speaks of the "souls of those who had been slain" in heaven (Revelation 6:9).

This is not, however, the natural condition of humans. So Paul can say that the final hope of believers is, "the redemption of our bodies" (Romans 8:23). He also says that he would rather not die and experience life separate from the body. Rather, he looks forward to the resurrection body, when body and 'soul' will be united together. So he says, "How we weary of our present bodies. That is why we look forward eagerly to the day when we shall have 'heavenly' bodies which we shall put on like new clothes. We shall not be merely spirits without bodies. These earthly bodies make us groan and sigh, but we don't really want to be spirits without bodies. What we want is to slip into our new bodies so that our dying bodies will be changed into immortal ones" (2 Corinthians 5:2-4).

All this will happen when Jesus comes back and "all the dead will hear His voice and come out of their graves" (John 5:28).

2) **God will judge all people.** Paul teaches that, "we will all stand before God's judgment seat" (Romans 14:10). This will happen when 'the Lord.... (comes) to judge everyone (Jude 14 & 15).

3) **The Church will be delivered.** The New Testament teaches that at the end the church will suffer great trial and "there will be great distress". However, "At that time they will see the Son of Man coming...with power and glory." This will be so that his people can "be with the Lord for ever" sharing His conquest of all his enemies. (Matthew 24:21,30,31 and 1 Thessalonians 4:17).

4) **The work of salvation will be completed.** Thus,

- Jesus will finally implement the victory which He won when He first came. John describes the time when this will happen in Revelation 5 and shows there that Jesus is able to bring to fulfilment God's salvation because he is the "Lamb who was slain" (See Revelation 5:6,9-10,12, 13).

- All God's enemies will be conquered once and for all. When this happens, says Paul, "then the saying that is written will come true, Death has been swallowed up in victory" (1 Corinthians 15:54). Together with death sin will also be defeated since, "the sting of death is sin ....But thanks be to God! He gives us the victory through the Lord Jesus Christ"(1 Corinthians 15:56). Together with death and sin the Devil himself will be finally defeated. John tells us that at the end, "the Devil (will be) thrown into Hell (and) tormented in judgment for ever" (Revelation 20:10).

- Then God's original purpose for Creation and Man will be finally achieved. At Jesus' return God will make "a new heaven and a new earth, the home of righteousness" (2 Peter 3:13); a world where the curse will be removed. (Revelation 22:3); where God will "live with humans" (Revelation 21:3 and compare Genesis 3:8) and where "there will be no more death or mourning or crying or pain, for the old order of things (will have passed away" (Revelation 21:4).

These great truths explain why:

- "We eagerly await a Saviour from heaven, the Lord Jesus Christ" (Philippians 3:20). The believers hopes are fixed upon the Lord's return and. our entire lives are to be governed by this hope.
- We are called to be watchful (Mark 13:37). We are to be vigilant in all that we do so that when he returns we shall be ready and prepared for Him and. He will not have to be ashamed of us.

But what will Jesus' return be like?

1) **It will be universally visible**. We are told, "every eye will see him" (Revelation 1:7). When Jesus first came it was very secret. Only a few knew and his life passed almost unnoticed by the vast mass of mankind. This will not be true when he comes again. One of the Bible words used to describe his return is 'parousia'. The word is found in Matthew 24:3; 1 Corinthians 15:23; 1 Thessalonians 2:19 and 2 Thessalonians 2:1,8. It is a word that describes the arrival of a great king. The New Testament tells us that he will come with great

glory and splendour.

2) **His return will be bodily**. The angels told the disciples, "This same Jesus, who has been taken bodily from you into heaven, will come back in the same way as you have seen him go" (Acts 1:11).

3) **His return will be final**. "Then the end will come" (1 Corinthians 15:24).

4) **His return will be a 'revelation'**. The Bible tells us that many things are true which do not seem to be so at the moment. Much of the Bible's message must be taken 'on trust' and by faith. However, the New Testament tells us that when Jesus comes again an 'apocalypse' and an 'epiphany' will take place. These words are found in 1 Corinthians 1:7 and 2 Thessalonians 2:8. They mean that those things that are now hidden will be fully revealed and that the veil will be drawn back from things so that things may be seen for what they truly are.

5) **His return will be sudden and unexpected**. Jesus said, "the Son of Man will come at a time when you do not expect him" (Matthew 24:44).

Point to Ponder

- All these things show why the Bible's teaching about the Second Coming of Jesus is so often repeated. Many Old Testament passages teach about Jesus' coming in glory (for example, Daniel 7:13, 14) as do over 250 passages in the New Testament. The doctrine is there in the Bible for all to see. Denial of the second coming is to deny the great hope of the Christian faith – and what a great hope it is!

10. We Believe in the Life to Come

The full display of God's salvation is still in the future and will be finally revealed when Jesus returns. But what happens in the meanwhile and what exactly will happen when he comes back?

What will happen when we die?

We have already seen that unless Jesus returns in the meanwhile all of us will die since God said to mankind, "Dust you are and to dust you will return" (Genesis 3:19). The reason for this is explained to us by Paul when he says, 'All have sinned' and, "The wages of sin is death" (Romans 3:23 & 6:23).

However, man was created immortal and it is God's intention that one day the mortality caused by sin will be "swallowed up" by immortality (1 Corinthians 15:53-54). This will be accomplished when the dead are raised to life.

Christians are, however, often confused as to what happens in the meanwhile. Nevertheless, a careful study of the Bible provides some clear guidelines for us.

1) The most important thing to say is that those who are Christians when they die will immediately be with Jesus. Thus Jesus could say to the dying thief, "This day you will be with me in Paradise" (Luke 23:43). Paul could also add, "I desire to depart (through death) and be with Christ, which is better by far" (Philippians 1:23) and speak of being, "away from the body and at home with the Lord" (2 Corinthians 5:8).

2) However, the 'dead' still await the full display of God's salvation. In the Old Testament 'death' was not the norm as far as God's ultimate purpose was concerned. God's blessing of his people was, "that you might live a long life" (Exodus 20:12). Thus, the Old Testament people did not look forward to death any more than we do (see Hezekiah in 2 Kings 20:1-6). They did believe they would be with God after death. As a result of Jesus' death and resurrection 'death' can be faced still more confidently: but still to be with Christ is not God's final purpose. So we read of the 'dead' in heaven crying out for the full salvation of God when they say, "How long, Sovereign Lord" (Revelation 6:9).

3) The Church is in a tension between the fact that the Kingdom of God has both arrived in Jesus and yet is not fully revealed. Even the 'dead' seem to experience the same tension in some way, longing for the redemption of their bodies.

There is no clear teaching as to what happens to the unbelieving dead. The Bible does seem to hint that they endure some anticipations of the torment in Hell.

What will the final judgment be like?

In both the Old and New Testaments God is described as one whose mercy and judgment is active in the present events and experiences of men and women. However, both Testaments also look to a final and complete reckoning in the age to come.

1) Thus, God is described as the one who, "defends the cause of the fatherless and the widow, and loves the foreigner, giving him food and clothing" (Deuteronomy 10:18). He is also described as one whose "wrath is being revealed from

heaven against all godlessness and wickedness of men" (Romans 1:18).

2) However, there is a day appointed for the final judgment. Thus, we read in Malachi, "Surely a day is coming, it will burn like a furnace. All the arrogant and every evildoer will be stubble, and that day that is coming will set them on fire......Not a root or a branch will be left of them" (4:l). Paul also speaks of, "God .....who will judge the living and the dead at Christ Jesus' appearing" (2 Timothy 4:1). Moreover, Jesus will execute the judgment of the Father since, "the Father.....has given Him authority to judge" (John 5:26-7).

3) All will be judged, even believers. This is true since, "All must appear before the judgment seat of Christ, that each one may receive what is due to him for the things done in the body" (2 Corinthians 5:10). This judgment cannot endanger the salvation of believers because, "there is now no condemnation to those who are in Christ Jesus" (Romans 8:1). His death will be credited to them. However, God's children will experience the judgment of a Father (1 Peter 1:17) who will examine how they have used their gifts, talents, opportunities and abilities in this life. This is taught in Luke 19:11-26 and 1 Corinthians 3:10-15. The believer's standing in the life to come will be based upon his or her faithfulness in this life. This is not, however, a reward: for no believer deserves any reward from God. It remains a gift of grace.

4) All others will be judged according to their works since, "God will give to each person according to what he has done" (Romans 2:6).

5) The standard of acceptance for all men is faith in Christ. The New Testament makes it clear that, "Salvation is found in no-one else, for there is no other name under heaven

given to men by which we must be saved" (Acts 4:12). Jesus himself said, "I am the way and the truth and the life. No-one comes to the Father except through me" (John 14:6). Apart from faith in Jesus all men stand condemned.

6) However, the Bible makes it clear that God will take into account the opportunities that men have had to hear the Gospel when he judges them. For some the judgment day will, accordingly, be "more bearable" than for others (Matthew 11:24).

The fact that apart from faith in Christ no one will enter God's Kingdom ought to drive us out in evangelism and mission.

What will the life to come be like?

1) The Bible begins its answer to this question by emphasising that there will be a division at the final judgment between Christians and all others. Daniel says, "those who sleep in the dust of the earth will awake: some to everlasting life, others to shame and everlasting contempt" (Daniel 12:2). Likewise Jesus taught of "a time corning when all who are in their graves win hear the Son of Man's voice and come out: those who have done good will rise to life and those who have done evil will rise to be condemned" (John 5:28-29).

2) The Bible teaches that there is a place to which the condemned will be sent; it is called Hell. Evangelical Christians are uncertain as to how to interpret the language about Hell. Clearly, to experience the punishment of God will be excruciating. However, they are divided as to whether the Bible implies the sufferings of Hell are eternal and whether, without experiencing salvation, all will be brought to a willing recognition of and worship of God.

What will happen to believers?

1) The final hope of believers is the New heavens and the New earth (See 2 Peter 3:13 and Isaiah 65:17 and 66:22. Thus, though it is true that the world "in its present form is passing away" (1 Corinthians 7:31) yet the Bible also teaches that the whole of the created order will be renewed in the final redemption (See Romans 8:19-25). Thus, there will be a real and continuing relationship between the world we know and the age to come. This is emphasised by the fact that there will be the same relationship between life as we know it now and the life of the new heavens and new earth. Our bodies will probably be like Jesus' resurrection body. They will have new properties and, above all, will be free from the effects of sin and death in living a perfect life.

2) In addition to this we can say that the age to come will be life in a perfect society in which each believer will have specific responsibilities. The effect of sin in the world was the disintegration of inter-personal relationships. But humans were created to live with and care for one another. Jesus broke down the divisions among us. Paul said, "He Himself is our peace...... and has broken the barrier, the dividing wall of hostility" (Ephesians 2:14). Thus: "There is neither Jew nor Greek, slave nor free, male nor female, for you are all one in Christ" (Galatians 3:28). This work of Jesus will be perfected in the age to come as the various pictures of the life to come emphasise, since they are all 'group' illustrations: a perfect city (Hebrews 13:14), a kingdom (Hebrews 12:28), a wedding feast (Revelation 19:17) etc.. There in society responsible service will be performed (Revelation 22:3) just as Adam worked in Eden (Genesis 2:15).

3) The life to come will be a God-centred life. The people of God will, at last, "see His face" (Revelation 22:4 and see also

1 John 3:23). This will be their greatest delight. The Psalmist said, "You will fill me with joy in your presence, with eternal pleasures at your right hand" (Psalm16:11).

The Believer's Hope

For the believer:

1) **Jesus' return is a 'blessed hope'** (Titus 2:13). In the middle of a hopeless world the believer knows that God remains Lord of his world and will achieve his purposes for it.

2) **Jesus' return gives great comfort in the face of death**. A Christian cannot grieve "like the rest of humanity, without hope" (1 Thessalonians 4:3). Of course, we hate death and dying because it is not 'natural' but the result of sin. The Christian also hates the separation caused by sin and grieves because of it. However, the fact that when Jesus comes believers, "will live together with him" (2 Corinthians 5:10) takes desolation away.

3) **Jesus' return should make the believer holy**. This is so since:

- A Christian is a citizen of the age to come ann. is called to evidence that citizenship now.
- A Christian will be holy in tie age to come. Believing this, "Everyone who has this hope in him, purifies himself" (1 John 3:2).
- One day the Christian will have to give account of his life to Jesus (2 Corinthians 5:10). With this in mind he or she should, out of love, "make every effort....to be holy" (Hebrews 12:14).

4) **Jesus' return should arouse believers to action:**

- To spread the Gospel: in order to warn men and women of the wrath of God to come upon all unbelievers. Jesus taught that "unless you repent, you too will perish" (Luke 13:5). The believer should also be zealous to spread the Gospel because the evangelisation of the world must take place before Jesus returns (Matthew 24:12).
- To build the Church. The Christian should seek to make the Church as holy as possible because it is the 'bride of Christ' which will one day be presented to him. The believer will do all that he or she can to ensure that the Church is ready when Jesus comes.
- To love and serve all men, showing to them the nature of the Kingdom and true citizenship of the age to come.
- Christians should pray for Jesus' return. Jesus himself taught believers to pray, "Your Kingdom come" (Matthew 6:10).

5) **Jesus' return ought to make Christians love one another.** The age to come will be an age of love but already, "God has poured out His love in our hearts" (Romans 5:5).

6) **Jesus' return should make believers watchful.**

7) **Jesus' return should make God's people 'a people of praise'.** The praise of heaven (Revelation 5:12ff; 7:10-12; 11:17-18; 15:3-4; 19:1-5) should be echoed on earth.

Point to Ponder

- What a hope... and what a challenge!

11. We Believe in the Call to a Holy Life

Being so loved by the triune LORD and with such a future before us, we should want to please him now and prepare to meet him.

The Spiritual Disciplines

1) God's purpose for us as Christians is that we come to 'share the divine nature' (2 Peter 1:4) and to experience intimacy and share fellowship with him and his Son. We are called into union with God. In so far as it is possible for human beings, we are to be 'carbon copies' of God himself, by his grace. This is why the Bible emphasises that we are indwelt by the Spirit of God. The LORD God, in the person of his Holy Spirit, comes to dwell within us. He, it is, who produces in the believer those things that characterise God himself. He produces holy desires and conforms us to the will of God in delighted obedience of God and humble and loving submission of one to another.

2) But to mature into such a relationship requires what are known as spiritual disciplines. The early Church, shortly after Pentecost, recognized this. We are told that they "devoted themselves to the apostles' teaching and the fellowship, to the breaking of bread and prayers" (Acts 2:32).

3) Thus, fundamental to spiritual growth is the fellowship of the church. This will be explored more fully below. However, it was clearly a recognized priority, and the reason is given, in the comment, "not neglecting to meet together,

as is the habit of some" but to "stir up one another to love and good works" (Hebrews 10:24,25). It explains the joy of the Psalmist when he says, "I was glad when they said to me, let us go to the house of the LORD' (Psalm 122:1).

4) The priority in meeting together was to listen to God, "the apostles' teaching". In the Old Testament, the spiritual life was seen nurtured by the person whose "delight is in the law of the LORD and who meditates on his law day and night" (Psalm 1:2). The longest Psalm (119) is wholly devoted to this theme. The delighted, devoted, ongoing, regular reading and reflection upon the words of the Bible lies at the heart of a growth into union with Christ: not least when God's people meet together. Interestingly, it was while Paul was leading a lengthy Bible study that the weary Eutychus fell asleep (Acts 20:9). However it is done, the Christian will want to find time to spend with an open Bible!

5) Listening to God is to be accompanied by responding to him: "and prayer". Prayer is where we speak to the LORD after we have heard from him. The prayers of the Bible are very varied, but they reflect the conversation of those with whom someone is intimate. Wordless fellowship, devotion and praise, requests for help, acknowledgement of failure and requests for forgiveness… these and others are found.

6) This is nurtured by the sacramental life of the Church: "the breaking of bread". This will be examined more below.

Point to Ponder

- If these are the means to our growth in grace, do they characterise our priorities and those of our churches? If not, why not?

12. We Believe that Christians' Responsibilities extend from Family to the Workplace and the World

Love for the LORD will affect the way we live in our families, relationships, workplaces and as citizens of the country to which we belong.

The Christian at home

1) Parents and Children

The Bible describes a number of responsibilities that parents are to exercise toward their children:

- **Parents are to provide materially for their children.** Paul says, "If anyone does not provide for his relatives, and especially for his immediate family, he has denied the faith and is worse than an unbeliever" (1 Timothy 5:8). A parent will be sensitive to the needs of his or her children and do everything possible to meet them.
- **Parents are to bring up their children in love.** They are to teach them to be disciplined. See Hebrews 12: 5-7. They are to show loving sensitivity to them so as to help their development to adulthood. In Colossians 3:21 we read, "Fathers, do not embitter your children, or they will become discouraged".

- **With this in mind Christian parents are to ensure that their children occupy a proper place in the home.** As they grow the children must be encouraged to make their own decisions and yet not be given responsibilities which they cannot carry. Children are to remain subordinate to their parents- but subordination is not the same as suppression.
- **Parents are to instruct their children in the Christian faith by life and example and teaching.** A godly example is to be accompanied by bringing "them up in the training and instruction of the LORD" (Ephesians 6:4).

2) Children and Parents

- **Children are to honour their parents.** They are to respect them as parents, even if they scarcely merit that respect. Compare Ephesians 6:2 with 1 Peter 2:18. The latter reference is to those in authority and naturally extends to parents.
- **Children are to receive instruction and discipline and not be rebellious.** See Hebrews 12:5-7 quoted above.
- **Children should provide for their parents when necessary.** We may not have asked to be born but that does not remove our responsibility toward those who reared us. Jesus roundly condemned those who sought to get out of this responsibility (Matthew 15: 4-6). 1 Timothy 5:8 which is quoted above applies just as much to children as to parents.

3) Husbands and Wives

- **Husbands and wives are to love one another.** Paul commands husbands to do so in Ephesians 5:25. We may assume that wives are to do the same. Paul shows what love means in practice in the following verses. It means to feed and care for one another just as much as for oneself. Mutual help and support and tender care (just like Jesus for us) are to characterise Christian marriages and are to be shown by a Christians spouse to the unbelieving partner (see 1 Peter 3:1, 2).

- **A godly example is to be shown to children.**

The Christian in the Workplace

1) When God created the world, He created men and women to work in it. In Genesis 1:28 we are told that God said, "Fill the earth and subdue it". Again, in Genesis 2:15 we read, "The LORD God took the man and put him in the Garden of Eden to work it and take care of it". So God created man to work.

2) In Genesis 3:17-19 we are told that sin has made work difficult. We read, "Cursed is the ground because of your sin; through painful toil you will eat of it all the days of your life. It will produce thorns and thistles for you   While the sweat of work is still on your forehead you will have to eat your food until you return to the ground...."

3) However, we are still expected to work within the framework of work and rest appointed by God who said, "Six days you shall labour" (Exodus 20:9).

The New Testament teaches the same truth very forcefully, "If a man will not work, he shall not eat" (2 Thessalonians 3:10).

4) What then is work? In our society we tend to think of work only as paid employment. However, in Bible times most work was not paid work at all. We need to think as the Bible

does: Work includes the studies of students, the non-paid labours of the voluntary helper, the considerable tasks of parents and homemakers as well as 'paid employment.

5) How should work be undertaken? The most important thing of all is that we work for God's glory. Paul said, "whatever you do, do it all for the glory of God" (1 Corinthians 10:31). Speaking of work, he said, "Serve wholeheartedly, as if you were serving the Lord" (Ephesians 6:7). We are to follow the example of Jesus (Matthew 20: 26-27). This means we will:

- **Work hard**. In Ecclesiastes 9:10 we are told, "Whatever your hand finds to do, do it with all your strength'".
- **Not be lazy**. See Proverbs 10:5.
- **Work cheerfully and not grudgingly**. "Serve wholeheartedly", said Paul (Ephesians 6:7).
- **Work hard even when the boss is not around**. See Ephesians 6:6.
- **Work to benefit others**. Paul told people to work, "doing something useful… (to) have something to share with those in need" (Ephesians 4:28). So we should work not merely to support ourselves.
- **Be respectful**. See 1 Peter 2:18 where we read, "submit yourselves to your masters with all respect good and harsh (ones)".

With these principles we can work out God's will for most of the situations which arise at work. However, with the Bible's view of work in mind we need to see that such principles apply just as much to the housewife or student.

6) What about the responsibilities of employers? We should notice that the Bible emphasises that a fair wage is to be paid (since a worker is worthy of his hire, Luke 10:7)) promptly and properly (see Leviticus 19:13). The modern attitude of

many employers that workers are like machines to be disposed of when they get older, or simply like any other capital resource is contrary to the thinking of the Bible. Everything cannot simply be reduced to the question, 'How much will it cost?'

We have already seen that a Christian is only truly a believer when the whole of his or her life is conformed to the will of God as it is revealed in the Bible.

The Christian and the State

1) At a time when the Roman Empire was ruled by a succession of bad rulers, Paul said, "Everyone must submit himself to the governing authorities" (Romans 13:1). The reason for this is that, "there is no authority except that which God has established. The authorities that exist have been established by God" (verses 1,2). This state of affairs "pleases God our Saviour, who wants all men to be saved' (1 Timothy 2:4). In a mysterious way God appoints government for the good of the Gospel. Because this is so, "he who rebels against authority is rebelling against what God has instituted, and those who do so will bring judgment upon themselves" (Romans 13:2).

2) Thus, Christians have an obligation to be good citizens. We are to show respect and honour and pay taxes and other revenue (Romans 13:6, 7). We are to pray for our rulers (1 Timothy 2:1, 2).

3) Thus, also, a Christian may accept public office and play his part in the affairs of the nation in so far as what he does is consistent with his Christian profession.

4) The State, however, has no right to interfere in the affairs of the churches when living in obedience to God. Thus the Church and individual believers must, in spiritual matters, obey God rather than any men. Jesus taught this in Matthew 22:21 when he said, "Give to Caesar what is Caesar's, and to God what is God's".

5) There can be no such thing, therefore, as a church established by the State for it is not able to make any decisions in this area. It is God alone who establishes His churches; He leads them in what they believe and how they are to conduct themselves and He gives His authority in these matters to no one else.

6) Equally, the church is not to be confused with the State. There can be no state religion for the state has no right to direct the consciences of men. A state should be pluralistic: that is, it should permit complete religious freedom. Moreover, a State cannot have a religion: only individuals can since the individuals religion is a matter of personal conscience.

7) Christian churches and individual Christian citizens may often seek to advise the state authorities of what God requires of men and women created in the image of God. The churches and individual believers will also preach the good news of Jesus to as many as possible of the citizens of the State. Moreover, a State may seek to protect and encourage true religion but this in no way justifies either a State religion or the binding of individual consciences.

8) The State may, however, act against a religious group which infringes the rights of the individual and the State. For example, a religious group may win adherents by the use of force or brainwashing. The State should act against such groups.

9) Sometimes a believer's responsibility to God is infringed by the State. In such circumstances the State is acting beyond its legitimate powers.

Point to Ponder

- Too often we think of the Christian faith in terms of our own belief in Jesus. However, to lay claim to believe him means we come to love him and delight in him and his ways… and this has implications for every area of our lives. Christians should be better husbands and wives, better parents, better workers and employers, better citizens…

13. We Believe in the Church and Its Privileges

Being a Christian means becoming a member of God's family, the Church. This brings with it tremendous privileges... and also responsibilities.

The Call to Commit Ourselves to One-Another

In 1 Corinthians 12:13 we read of every true believer, "For we were all baptised by one Spirit into one body" This teaches two things:

1) That every true believer has received the Holy Spirit at conversion and in this way have been united to Christ;

2) That the life which the Holy Spirit gives is, inescapably, corporate: body-life which, as the subsequent verses show, is expressed together with others who have the same faith. This confirms an impression which may be gained from reading the Bible: that a truly Christian life is always corporate. Thus:

3) God's purpose for mankind is corporate. In Genesis 2:18 we read that, "The LORD God said, "It is not good for man to be alone". This is because mankind is made in the image of God: and God is 'corporate'. Thus we read, 'Let us make man in our own image."

4) God's purpose for redeemed mankind is corporate. In the Old Testament the people of God are called a "community" (Exodus 35:1 and many other passages) and in the New

Testament the word 'church' is used of them. This word has the same meaning as 'community'. It emphasises that God's people are those who assemble together.

5) The believer's hope is corporate. In the future the people of God will be a "city" (Revelation 21:1-4). Many of the words used in the Bible of the people of God are words which emphasise this same point. Thus they are a:

- "people" (Exodus 6:7);
- "body" (1 Corinthians 12:13);
- "building" (1 Corinthians 3:16);
- "kingdom" (Colossians 1:13);
- "family" (Ephesians 2:19).

6) Thus, while all true believers are 'the church', yet the New Testament makes it quite clear that such believers will inevitably seek to express the reality of this fact by committing themselves to one another in local churches. This explains why Luke emphasises that the early believers were "together" (Acts 2:44). Thus, the New Testament has no place for the 'solitary' believer who avoids contact with other believers.

The character of a local church's life

The character of the life of a local church is seen in several ways:

1) In the basic convictions which unite its members and form the basis for all its actions. A true believer is someone who is no longer his or her own master or mistress. A believer has been "bought with a price" the price of Jesus' own death. His or her whole responsibility is now to "honour God" (1 Corinthians 6:20).

2) In particular, this now means that the Lord Jesus has absolute authority over the believer and over all God's people. This is why Paul so often described himself as a "servant" of Jesus (see, for example, Romans 1:1) for a servant does not have any personal rights but must always do that which the master requires. What was true for Paul is true of every believer.

3) This authority is seen to extend to everything which the local church does when we note that the church is described as a "body" in which Jesus is the head who governs the conduct of all the members. This thought is very clearly expressed in Ephesians 4 and 1 Corinthians 12.

4) Thus we see that the local church, and every member in it, is to be motivated by the desire to do what Jesus wants. Consequently, every decision taken in a local church is not so much governed by the majority view of the members (which may well be wrong) but by the mind of Jesus (Acts 13:1-4; 15:28-31; 1 Corinthians 5:4-5).

Where, then, do we find Jesus' will for the local church?

1) The answer is a simple one: in the authoritative Scriptures which look forward to (Old Testament), describe the life and work of (Gospels) and reflect upon (Acts-Revelation) Jesus. Thus all true believers will be like the Bereans who "examined the Scriptures every day" (Acts 17:11) in order to find and do the will of Jesus. Nothing, whether personal prejudice or whim, or convention of the church or past traditions, must be allowed to over-rule the Bible. All people and everything must bow before the absolute authority of Jesus revealed in the Bible.

2) One final thing needs to be said here. To understand the Bible correctly we need the Holy Spirit to lead us (John 14:26). Thus true believers and true church's will be convinced that everything they do must be governed by the absolute authority of Jesus, revealed in the Bible through the assistance of the Holy Spirit.

Shared Attitudes

1) One of the greatest truths in the Bible is the one which teaches us that when we become true believers in Jesus all the traditional racial, class, sexual, educational and other barriers which divide men and women from one another in the world are demolished. Our unity in Jesus breaks all the other walls down. Thus, Paul tells us: "For Jesus himself is our peace, who has made the two one and has destroyed the barrier, the dividing wall of hostility (therefore) there is neither Jew nor Greek (racial, religious and educational divisions) slave nor free (class distinctives) male nor female, for you are all one in Christ" (Ephesians 2:14 and Galatians 3:28).

2) Thus, when we read the New Testament we notice that it was marked by a unity which (usually) overcame these other differences that ungodly people make so much of. This is seen in Acts 2:44 where we read that the early believers "were together".

- This unity is something which should mark the life of every true church and should be jealously guarded. Paul said, "Make every effort to keep the unity of the Spirit through the bond of peace" (Ephesians 4:3).
- The reason that we need to guard our unity is that we remain very different sorts of people: we have different personalities and interests. This can so often lead to

conflict: and there is nothing that the Devil delights in more than a divided church since a divided church denies the very Gospel it proclaims.

3) It may seem to be impossible to maintain the high standards of the Bible: indeed many Christians seem to have given up any attempt to ensure their churches are what they should be. But we shouldn't despair because if we are true believers we now live in the realm of the supernatural where the impossible can be attained with God's help. This is exactly what the Bible teaches. We are told that God gives 'spiritual fruit' or 'graces' to all believers to enable them to live up to His high standards. These graces are all things which help us live together in unity: love, joy, peace, patience, kindness, goodness, faithfulness, gentleness, self-control (see Galatians 5:22-23; Philippians 4:8-9, etc.). They are to be cultivated in fellowship in order for us to keep and increase our unity. Thus, no Christian has any excuse for being divisive. The resources are available. The church can live and manifest such a life-style as is impossible in the sinful world. It also follows that every effort must be made to discipline those in a fellowship who seek to undermine this precious gift from God.

Mutual Responsibilities

All the members will be seen active in meeting their responsibilities within the corporate life of the church.

There are a number of such responsibilities:

1) The members of a Christian fellowship are to give the highest possible priority to all the meetings of the church. This is commanded in the Bible. The writer to the Hebrews says, "Let us not give up meeting together, as some are in the

habit of doing" (Hebrews 10:25). But it is not just commanded: it is taught for our own good since that same verse continues, "but let us encourage one another". In other words we are to meet together because we shall find our faith strengthened by doing so. But when we do not do so we are in danger of letting our faith shrivel up and die.

2) The members are also to expend every effort to preserve the unity of the church. First, they must all guard their own hearts and then, secondly, seek to do all that they can to ensure that the cancer of division is not allowed to take root elsewhere.

3) The members will seek to show mutual love and care for all their brothers and sisters in Christ. Jesus said, "Love one another, as I have loved you" (John 13: 34). These words emphasise the obligation and the way in which true believers are to show that love. Jesus loved even the unlovely and did everything possible (on the Cross) to meet their every need. This sacrificial love the true believer has the responsibility to show to everyone in a local church. In the early church this was shown in mutual sharing (Acts 4:44), in hospitality (Acts 4:46) etc. Our time, money and abilities are to be used for the benefit of others in the local church.

4) The members of the local church have a financial respon-sibility to the local church. In the Old Testament God's people were required to set aside a tenth of their income to support the work of the priests (Numbers 18:24-28). In the New Testament true believers are expected to give freely and without grudging (2 Corinthians 9:5,7), regularly (1 Corinthians 16:2), for the support of those who "labour in the word" (Galatians 6:6; 1 Timothy 5:17), for the relief of the needs of God's people (Romans 15:25 and the following verses; Acts 6:1-7) and any other needs.

Some believe that the 'tenth' is still commanded for us today. Others believe that there is personal freedom to determine how much is given (2 Corinthians 9:7) but that the standard of such giving is to be sacrificial. Poverty of giving reflects a lack of love for Jesus: such can only reflect back upon one's own spiritual life and impoverish it (2 Corinthians 9:6).

5) The members of the local church will encourage and be actively involved in helping the church meet its own responsibilities (see further below).

6) The members of the local church will desire and encourage the recognition and use of spiritual gifts for the building up of the church. When the Holy Spirit comes to live in the believer at conversion he gives each one a gift or gifts to use for the benefit of the local fellowship (1 Corinthians 12:7). These gifts vary very considerably. Some are natural abilities which God now uses for his own glory; some seem especially 'supernatural'. All this is, however, only our way of looking at things. God regards all these things as spiritual gifts and however important or unimportant they seem to us they are all necessary for the spiritual growth of the local church. Indeed those that might seem least important are often the most vital for the smooth running of a local church. Paul emphasises this in 1 Corinthians 12:14-31.

Every believer ought to seek to find out what gifts they have and seek new gifts (1 Corinthians 14:1). No-one should despise their own gifts or be jealous of other people's gifts. Neither should any believer neglect to use the gift(s) they have- for this is to rob the local church Rather, in meeting regularly with others they will exercise them so that the church may be edified.

7) All believers in a local church have a responsibility to live a consistent life in society and the home.

8) All believers in a local church must show a teachable, submissive spirit. Paul says, "submit to one another out of reverence to Christ" (Ephesians 5:21). All believers will be ready to learn, not to insist on their own way, deferring to others. This respect should especially be shown to the leaders of the local church (Hebrews 13:17).

Point to Ponder

- Every true believer is to seek to meet these responsibilities with every ability and grace that has been given to them: looking to God for all the resources they need. As they meet the responsibilities they will also find that their spiritual life will be greatly enriched to their own blessing and to the glory of Jesus.

14. We Believe in the Church and its Sacraments

The life of the Church and all its members is grounded in and nurtured by the sacraments of Baptism and the Lord's Supper.

Christian Baptism

Baptism was an essential part of both the teaching and practice of the New Testament churches. Thus:

1) **The Teaching of the New Testament**. Jesus commanded baptism (Matthew 28:19); the early Christians taught it (Acts 2:38, 22:16) and the early letters which Christians wrote also speak of it (Romans 6:4; Colossians 2:12; 1 Peter 3:21; Hebrews 6:2).

2) **The Practice of the New Testament**. Jesus was baptised (Matthew 3:13-17) "to do everything that was right". He was obedient to all the requirements which govern us. The disciples and the early churches followed the example of Jesus (John 4:2; Acts 2:41; 8:12 & 38; 9:18; 10:48; 16:15 & 33; 18:8 and 19:5). In 1 Corinthians 1:13-16 Paul assumes that all the early Christians were baptised. Indeed, the New Testament knows of no such thing as an unbaptised Christian. The reason for this lies in the fact that:

Baptism is the profession of faith in the New Testament.

It is very clear that the response which the early churches expected when people came to faith in Jesus was that they sought baptism. When the good news of Jesus was proclaimed men and women were called to respond in baptism (Acts 2:38). Baptism was the response to the good news. This is why the New Testament often seems to speak of faith and baptism interchangeably- true faith was faith expressed in baptism.

The Importance of Baptism

The New Testament also places emphasis on baptism because it demonstrates our conversion, and is a declaration of ownership and a pledge of obedience.

1) **Baptism demonstrates our conversion**. It is a picture of our spiritual death and resurrection with Christ. Paul teaches this in Romans 6:3-4 and Colossians 2:12. It is also a picture of our new relationship with God. Sins are washed away by faith expressed in baptism (Acts 22:16); our hearts are now clean (Hebrews 10:22) and our consciences clear (1 Peter 3:21). Finally, behind all this, baptism is a picture of our receiving the Holy Spirit. This is very clear in Acts 2:38 where those who respond in repentance and baptism are promised the Holy Spirit.

2) **Baptism is a statement of ownership**. Baptism is a clear command of Jesus and the apostles (Matthew 28:19; Acts 2:38). In Luke 7:29-30 we are told that certain people "rejected God's purpose for themselves, because they had not been baptized".

In fact, baptism is the first expression of our obedience to Jesus which itself itself shows the genuineness of our faith and repentance. If we have truly repented we are no longer our own "we are bought with a price". We are slaves to Jesus (see studies above) and we obey Him in baptism.

3) **Baptism is a pledge of obedience.** In the New Testament baptism is a baptism of repentance (Matthew 3:11 and Acts 2:38). Thus, just as there are fruits or evidences of repentance (Matthew 3:8) so, in baptism, we pledge to live a life of holiness in the image of Jesus.

In view of all this teaching it is not surprising to find that the New Testament makes it very clear that baptism is the means of entry into the local church. Thus, we find that in the early church it was those who had responded to the good news in the way that God had appointed who were welcomed into the local church (Acts 2:41). Their public statement in baptism that they were the disciples of Jesus was the recognised means of entry into the membership of the local church: with all its privileges and responsibilities.

The 'Lord's Table'

The Lord's Table can be viewed in a number of different ways. It:

1) **Looks back.** Paul tells us this in 1 Corinthians 11:24 when he tells us that Jesus said "Do this in remembrance of me". The Lord's Table is, therefore, a memorial service.

   What do we remember? Paul tells us. "You proclaim the Lord's death", he says, (see 1 Corinthians 11:26). In other words, we celebrate the self-offering of Jesus as the substitute for sinners who were under the wrath of God.

2) **Looks forward.** Paul says, "You proclaim the Lord's death until He comes" (1 Corinthians 11:26). It is a temporary celebration, until all the fruits of Jesus' death are ours when he comes again. Thus when we meet we remember with awe and joy both what he has and will yet do for us.

3) **Looks outward.** Paul tells us in 1 Corinthians 10:16-17, "Is not the cup of thanksgiving for which we give thanks a fellowship in the blood of Christ? And is not the bread that we break a fellowship in the body of Christ? Because there is one loaf, we, who are many, are one body, for we all partake of the one loaf". Paul tells us here that in meeting at the Lord's Table we do not so much remember that we, individually, are Christians but that we, together, are members together of the Christian community. In this way we are reminded of our responsibilities to one another.

The same passage speaks of the Lord's Table as "communion" or fellowship. In a way that we cannot put into words, sharing in 'communion' deepens and nurtures our relationship with Jesus.

Who should attend the Lord's Table?

1) In New Testament times there were no such persons as unbaptised believers: those who were converted were signed and sealed into their faith through baptism and into the privileges and responsibilities of a local church. One of the privileges that the members of local churches enjoyed was access to the Lord's Table.

2) The reason for this is obvious. Baptism is the declaration that we have 'put on Christ', it is the response of faith. The Lord's Table is the 'meal' that symbolises our continuing fellowship with Jesus and His people.

3) Biblically speaking, the people who have both a right and an obligation to attend the celebration of the Lord's Table are the baptised members of the local church (who are not under discipline).

How should we celebrate the Lord's Table?

1) **Simply**. The original meal was a simple unadorned meal (we read about it in Matthew 26:17-30; Mark 14:12-26; Luke 22:7-38 and 1 Corinthians 11:17-33). This ensured that the important lessons which it was intended to teach were not lost sight of: we should surely follow such an example and, especially, give close attention to the instructions of Paul in 1 Corinthians.

2) **Regularly**. No detailed instructions are given in the Bible as to when and how often we should meet for the Lord's Table. All that is clear is that it took place regularly. In doing this the foundations of the Christian faith were repeatedly emphasised so that no believer could ever lose sight of them. We should be guided by such thinking.

3) **With one loaf and one cup**. This was obviously the New Testament practice as the references given above indicate. The sharing of one cup and one loaf emphasised that in meeting around the Lord's Table those who met recognised that they were members of one another through Jesus' death.

4) **Thoughtfully**. In 1 Corinthians 11:28 we are told to "examine ourselves" before we meet together. Paul explains what he means when he says that we should not come "without recognising the body of the Lord". In other words we are to remember what we are doing: declaring our faith in Jesus as our Lord and Saviour.

In this passage, Paul uses the language of blessing and curse. He warns that if we do not come in the proper way we will suffer for it. The opposite is also assumed to be true: when we do come properly we will receive the Lord's blessing.

Thus we need to be sure that we do come and that we come properly.

Point to Ponder

- A truly Christian life feeds and grows as the sacraments are obediently and (in the case of the Lord's Table) regularly celebrated. A genuine Church will seek to promote such life by a proper use of the sacraments.

15. We Believe in the Church and its Ministries

The local church is the place where those who have placed themselves under the authority of Jesus and the Scriptures seek to live as the LORD commands.

Authority in the Church

Where is authority found in the local church and how is this authority outworked in the activities of the fellowship?

In the Old Testament:

1) **The people of God were a 'theocracy'.** This meant that the final rule and authority was God's - and his alone.

2) **The leadership of God's people was essentially by 'charismatic' leaders.** Leadership of God's people was by men and women who had been called and equipped by God. God's people had a responsibility to recognise these gifted people and to follow their lead.

3) **Leadership involved being servants of all God's people,** in giving a godly example for all to follow.

These emphases reappear in the New Testament in the teaching given about the church: the New Testament people of God. Thus we note:

1) **The final authority and rule of the church lies in the hands of the Lord Jesus Christ.** Thus Paul says, "he is the head of the body, the church   so that in everything He

might have the supremacy" (Colossians 1:18). Paul also says, "God placed all things under his feet and appointed him to be head over everything for the church" (Ephesians 1:22). This means that every debate and decision taken in the local church is not so much an attempt to discover the majority opinion (which may well be wrong) as to find the mind of Christ. When His mind is clear the church is to obey. Thus in Acts 13:1-4 we read of one group of believers who knew the will of the Lord and obeyed it. In Acts 15:28-31 we have described for us how the church was guided by the Holy Spirit to make a decision.

In the New Testament various methods, appropriate to each situation and issue, were used to find the Lord's will. Common to all of them is that it was as the local church gathered together they found His will. The will of God for the church is not found by individuals acting on their own opinions and whims. It is found when the church together seeks that will.

2) **God provides people who He has qualified to guide and lead and serve the church**. Paul says, "When Jesus ascended on high He. .. .gave gifts to men   so that the body of Christ . . .be built up ... He gave ... evangelists, pastors and teachers" (Ephesians 4: 8,12,11). These gifted people have a God-given authority to lead His people. It is the local church's responsibility to recognise those who God has equipped and obey them. The writer to the Hebrews says, "Obey your leaders and submit to their authority" (Hebrews 13:17).

3) However, it is important to notice that **although the Lord gives gifts it is the responsibility of the church to recognise and appoint them**. Thus, the authority of such leaders depends upon the recognition of the church. A church may suffer where it does not recognise the gifts God

has given to it- but those thus gifted have no right to exercise a calling which the church does not recognise. It is also important that every church be on a constant look out to discern the gifts which God has given.

4) Thus **there are three 'authorities' in the local church**: the supreme authority of Christ, the authority of the local church when gathered (see especially 1 Corinthians 5:4-5) and the authority of those gifted by God to lead. These three authorities ought to interact and overlap in a local church. The leaders and the church cannot claim an authority that is Christ's. The leaders cannot dictate to the church: they can only warn where necessary and must always be ready to be corrected by the local church when gathered on the basis of the Scripture. Moreover, while a good leadership will be often advising and encouraging the church on a wide range of issues, ultimate responsibility for raising matters and implementing them lies with the gathered church.

What should the local church do when it meets together?

In answering this question we should notice two things:

1) **Few rules are given in the Bible to guide the conduct of the church**. Rather the Holy Spirit is given to His people (especially when they are together) to lead the church. Freely following the Spirit the Church finds out what it should do.

2) **Certain principles are provided within which the Spirit's freedom is to be expressed**. Thus four corporate responsibilities are commanded of the local church: worship, fellowship, ministry and witness. We shall see what the Bible says about each of these responsibilities.

orship

Worship is frequently described in the Bible. In the Old Testament it is especially found in the Psalms, 'the hymnbook of the Old Testament people of God'.

2) **The New Testament is also full of expressions of worship.** We read of its practice in Matthew 6:9; Mark 14:12,13; Luke 1:46-55, 68-79, 2:14, 29-32, 4:16; Acts 3:1,2, 4:24,25 etc.. Several 'doxologies' are quoted (Romans 11:33-36; 16:27; 1 Timothy 1:17; 6:15,16; Jude 24,25; Revelation 1:5,6. Lines from early Christian hymns are found (Ephesians 5:14; Philippians 2:5-11; Colossians 1:15-20; 1 Timothy 3:16). Other phrases from the churches worship are found in 1 Corinthians 16:22; Romans 1:25, 8:15.

3) **Worship is a fundamental feature of heaven** (Revelation 4:8-11, 5:11-14 and 7:9-12).

4) **All this emphasises the responsibility of all of God's people to regularly join together and 'continually offer to God praise'** (Hebrews 13:15). To 'offer worship' really has the meaning 'serve' or 'minister'. This is important. Very often Christians come to worship together thinking, 'What will I get out of this' rather than saying 'what can I give to God in this?'

5) Thus **every Christian who is not spiritually sick will want to obey God and together with other believers to worship him.**

What items are included in 'worship'? Several are indicated in the Bible:

- **Praise, especially in song.** Paul tells us this in Ephesians 5:19 and Colossians 3:16. We are to sing joyfully together because of all God's goodness to us.

79

The love of a congregation for the Lord may often be judged by the singing!

- **Prayer**. Wherever the New Testament churches met together they joined in prayer.
- **Giving**. 1 Corinthians 16:1-4 indicates that the giving of the church was associated with their worship meetings.
- **The Lord's Table**.
- **Study of God's Word**. In the worship of the early church the Scriptures were read (Colossians 4:16) after the pattern of the Old Testament people of God (Nehemiah 8:5-8). The reading was accompanied by an explanation (Acts 2:42 and 6:2). This could be a sermon but often it was undertaken through discussion (Acts 20:9 is literally "dialogued"). It involved those especially gifted for Bible teaching but could include contributions from others (1 Corinthians 1:26).

Guided by the Holy Spirit each congregation will seek to worship in such a way that all these various elements are included in a properly balanced way.

How should we worship?

1) **Recognising that the risen Lord Jesus is present**.

2) **Looking to the Holy Spirit's ministry as he gives us power to worship** (Philippians 3:3; John 4:24) and makes it real (1 Corinthians 12:3). He checks unworthy instincts (1 Corinthians 14:40), inspires prayer (Romans 8:26, 27), arouses praise (Ephesians 5:18,19), leads into truth (1 Corinthians 2:10-13), gives gifts (Romans 12:4-8) and convicts unbelievers (John 6:8; 1 Corinthians 14:24).

3) **Governed by mutual love and a desire to build up one another** (Ephesians 4:12-16).

With these principles there is tremendous scope for variety as the Holy Spirit leads each congregation.

Fellowship

1) **'Love' was an essential part of the life of the early church.** God loves His people and therefore they love one another (John 3:34, 35). In the 'fellowship' that results, God is glorified Romans 15:7) and the success of the Gospel guaranteed (John 17:23, 3:34).

2) **This love leading to fellowship leads to self-giving to one another** (1 Corinthians 13; 1 John 3:16). A 'Calvary love' that stoops to those in need, is forgiving and patient is the result. It is the great gift of the Spirit producing that which is humanly impossible.

3) **This love is not simply a warm feeling but is very practical.** Look up Hebrews 13:2: 1 Peter 4:9; Galatians 6:2, Hebrews 10:25; Philippians 1:9-11; 1 Corinthians 10:16, 17. These verses teach us that love inspired fellowship is to be seen in giving hospitality, bearing one another's burdens, encouraging and praying for one another and especially being united at the Lord's Table.

Every true church will always be seeking to foster and increase such practical fellowship among its members.

Ministry

1) **Jesus came as a servant.** He expects his people to follow him and to find true greatness in doing so (Mark 9:33-37; Luke 22:24-27).

2) **To help believers to meet their responsibility he gives gifts to each one.** These gifts vary enormously (Romans 12:3-8; 1 Corinthians 12:7-11; Ephesians 4:7,16; 1 Peter

4:10) but they are all given to help us serve one another and glorify Jesus.

Witness

1) While every individual believer is called to witness to friends, family, workmates and neighbours **the responsibility for witness is above all that of the local church**. This responsibility began with the apostles (Acts 1:8) and continues as our responsibility today.

2) **Witness includes all the words and actions which bring men and women face to face with the Gospel.**

3) **Such witness involves our effort, prayers and gifts.** It is not to be left to certain members of the church.

4) **Every true church will always be exploring ways to bring the Gospel of the Lord Jesus to those in need.**

The local church and other local churches

New Testament local churches had full authority to seek the mind of the Lord Jesus and organise themselves according to His will for them. With the possible exception of the unique ministry of the apostles there were no persons or organisations who had such an authority over local churches so as to dictate to them what they should do.

However, we do notice that:

1) As the situation required, they met together or sent messengers to one another to deal with common problems or needs and to make decisions together. We find a very good example of this in Acts 15.

2) They showed a practical and living concern for one another. They acted together for certain common ends (2 Corinthians 8:19) and gave help to those in need (Romans 15:26), they received one another (Romans 16:1,2), shared news (2 Corinthians 8) and apostolic letters (Colossians 4:16) etc.. Paul could speak of the daily burden which he had for all the churches (2 Corinthians 11:28) and seemed to be active in encouraging others to feel the same concern.

3) The motive for acting in such a way was, apparently, a desire to show the visible unity of God's people which had so concerned Jesus in His prayer in John 17 (see, especially verses 20 and following).

Point to Ponder

- Being a Christian or 'worshipping the triune God' is an incredible privilege but requires wholehearted commitment, overflowing love and a transformed lifestyle nurtured and witnessed through the corporate life of the Church.

Note: No one version of the English Bible is used in these studies. Sometimes passages are paraphrased and do not follow any one version (though they seek to be faithful to the original Hebrew and Greek in which the Bible books were originally written). They are selected to best make the point that is being discussed.